Sd.Kfz.166 Sturmpanzer „Brummbär"

Volume 1

Waldemar Trojca
Markus Jaugitz

J.J. Fedorowicz Publishing

Published by J.J. Fedorowicz Publishing, Inc.,
104 Browning Boulevard, Winnipeg, Manitoba, Canada R3K 0L7
Tel: (204) 837-6080, Fax: (204) 889-1960,
e-mail: jjfpub@jjfpub.mb.ca, web: www.jjfpub.mb.ca

Series design & layout: Waldemar Trojca
Cover designed by: Waldemar Trojca
Color plates designed by: Waldemar Trojca
Color plates and cover artwork by: Zbigniew Kolacha
DTP: Andrzej Szewczyk
Scanning of the photographs: Waldemar Trojca
Photographs reworked digitally by Andrzej Szewczyk
Proofreading: Agnieszka Klepacka, Andrzej Szewczyk, Jerzy Jóźwik
Text, color profiles, line drawings and photos are copyright Waldemar Trojca (© TROJCA)
Printed by: Małopolska Poligrafia s.c., ul. Zawiła 69, 30-390 Kraków POLAND

Printed in Poland
ISBN 0-921991-64-9

Other Titles by J.J. Fedorowicz Publishing

The Leibstandarte (1. SS-Panzer-Division):
  Volumes I, II, III, IV/1 and IV/2
European Volunteers (5. SS-Panzer-Division)
Das Reich (2. SS-Panzer-Division):
  Volumes I and II
The History of Panzer-Korps "Großdeutschland":
  Volumes 1, 2 and 3
The History of the 7. SS-Mountain-Division "Prinz Eugen"
Otto Weidinger
Otto Kumm
Manhay, The Ardennes: Christmas 1944
Armor Battles of the Waffen-SS, 1943-1945
Tiger: The History of a Legendary Weapon,
  1942-1945
Hitler Moves East
Tigers in the Mud
Panzer Aces
Footsteps of the Hunter
History of the 12. SS-Panzer-Division
  "Hitlerjugend"
Grenadiers, the Autobiography of Kurt Meyer
Field Uniforms of German Army Panzer Forces
  in World War 2
Tigers in Combat, Volumes I and II
Infanterie Aces
Freineaux and Lamormenil-The Ardennes
The Caucasus and the Oil
East Front Drama-1944
The History of the Fallschirm-Panzer-Korps
  "Hermann Göring"
Michael Wittmann and the Tiger Commanders
  of the Leibstandarte
The Western Front 1944:
  Memoirs of a Panzer Lehr Officer

Luftwaffe Aces
Quiet Flows the Rhine
Decision in the Ukraine: Summer 1943
Combat History of the Schwere Panzer-Jäger-
  Abteilung 653
The Brandenburgers - Global Mission
Field Uniforms of Germany's Panzer Elite
Soldiers of the Waffen-SS:
  Many Nations, One Motto
In the Firestorm of the Last Years of the War
The Meuse First and Then Antwerp
Jochen Peiper: Commander, Panzer-Regiment
  "Leibstandarte"
Sturmgeschütze vor! Assault Guns to the Front!
Karl Baur: A Pilot's Pilot
Kharkov
Panzer Aces 2
Panzertaktik
The History of Panzerregiment
  "Großdeutschland"
Combat History of Sturmgeschütz-Brigade 276
Normandy 1944: German Military Organization
  Combat Power and Organizational
  Effectiveness
The Combat History of schwere Panzer-Abteilung 503
Funklenkpanzer: A History of German Army Remote-
  and Radio-Controlled Armor Units
The Combat History of schwere Panzer-Abteilung 508,
  In Action in Italy with the Tiger I
Tragedy of the Faithful: A History of the
  III. (germanisches) SS-Panzer-Korps
Waldemar Trojca Markus Jaugitz,
  Sd. Kfz. 166 Sturmpanzer "Brummbär" Volumes 1

In Preparation:

The Combat History of schwere Panzer-Jäger-Abteilung 654
Kursk, A Photo History of the Epic Battle (Volume 1: The North)
Kursk, A Photo History of the Epic Battle (Volume 2: The South)
Kursk: A Text History (Franz Kurowski)

Overview

As early as 1935 the chief of the operations section of the *Oberkommando des Heeres* (Army High Command), the eventual *Generalfeldmarschall* von Manstein, suggested in a memorandum that field pieces be employed on armored chassis to support infantry. The term *Sturmartillerie* (assault artillery) was coined in this memorandum.

In contrast to tanks, these self-propelled guns would advance with the infantry and engage dangerous targets in a direct-fire mode. They were also supposed to be employed as a defense against armored attacks.

The vehicle discussed in the memorandum lead to the development of the *Sturmgeschütz* (assault gun). This development satisfied one of the requirements identified by the infantry as necessary for its employment on the modern battlefield.

The campaign in Poland in September 1939 had demonstrated that it was difficult for the motorized artillery battalions and the motorized infantry-gun companies of the *Panzer-Divisionen* to keep pace with the tempo of the tanks.

Much consideration was given to developments that led to placing an infantry gun on a self-propelled chassis. In the course of these developments, the 15 cm *schweres Infanterie-Geschütz 33*, which had been introduced in 1927 to field units, was installed on the chassis of a *Panzer I, Ausführung B*.

After the trials had been completed in January 1940, a total of 38 vehicles of that type were converted by April 1940. Six guns were consolidated into each *Infanteriegeschütz-Kompanie (mot S.)* - infantry-gun company (self-propelled) - and issued to six different *Panzer-Divisionen*.

Infantry-Gun Company Designation	Panzer-Division
schwere Infanteriegeschütz-Kompanie (mot. S.) 701	*9. Panzer-Division*
schwere Infanteriegeschütz-Kompanie (mot. S.) 702	*1. Panzer-Division*
schwere Infanteriegeschütz-Kompanie (mot. S.) 703	*2. Panzer-Division*
schwere Infanteriegeschütz-Kompanie (mot. S.) 704	*5. Panzer-Division*
schwere Infanteriegeschütz-Kompanie (mot. S.) 705	*7. Panzer-Division*
schwere Infanteriegeschütz-Kompanie (mot. S.) 706	*10. Panzer-Division*

These vehicles received their baptism of fire during the French Campaign in May 1940, just like their *Sturmgeschütz* counterparts.

A replacement version of the vehicle was converted as early as October 1940 using the *sIG 33* on the chassis of a *Panzer II*. After trials, a number of changed were requested, which were incorporated into the pre-production series of vehicles. The Alkett firm completed 12 of them in the winter of 1941/42, where the infantry gun was incorporated into a longer and wider *Panzer II* chassis.

With six guns issued per company, the newly formed *schwere Infanteriegeschütz-Kompanie (mot.S.) 707 (Schützen-Regiment 155)* and *schwere Infanteriegeschütz-Kompanie (mot.S.) 708 (Schützen-Regiment 200)* became part of the *90. leichte Afrika-Division*.

At that point, the self-propelled guns were still employed purely as support vehicles for the infantry and the *Panzergrenadiere* (mechanized infantry). As a result of the changing situation at the front, however, the requirements for the vehicles started to change. These changing requirements were determined during a *Führer* conference held from 10-22 September 1942:

The clear necessity has developed during the fighting in Stalingrad to have a heavy field piece in a heavily armored vehicle that can deliver rounds that have a "mine-like" effect that can destroy entire buildings with one or two rounds. It is not important whether the firing is done at great ranges or the vehicle can move rapidly. On the contrary, what is decisively important is good armor protection. Everything possible must be done to create a minimum of 6 and, if possible, a total of 12 such vehicles within the next fourteen days. If the incorporation of a *sIG* into the turret of a *Panzer III* or *Panzer IV* is not possible, then it must be attempted to place that gun into the chassis of a *Sturmgeschütz*.

By October 1942 12 *sIG* had been incorporated into a casemate-like superstructure of a *Panzer III* chassis. These vehicles received the designation of *15 cm Sturm-Infanteriegeschütz 33*. In all, twenty-four of those vehicles were ordered. Six each of the vehicles were issued to *Sturmgeschütz-Abteilung 177* (177th Assault Gun Battalion) and *Sturmgeschütz-Abteilung 244*. The remaining twelve went to the *Sturm-Infanteriegeschütz-Kompanie* of *Lehr-Bataillon XVII* (Instruction battalion XVII).

Independent of the development of a vehicle based on the *Panzer III* chassis, Alkett presented Hitler with the designs for a *sIG* on a *Panzer IV* chassis in October 1942. Hitler thereupon requested to be informed as soon as possible of production timelines for 40 to 60 of these vehicles, to include the development of the new armament required for it. It was imperative that the newly developed 15 cm *sIG* be capable of firing thin-walled casings with a high-explosive effect suitable for fighting in built-up areas.

At the time the contract was awarded, there were production bottlenecks. As a result and among other measures, it was ordered that the chassis of repaired vehicles be used. At the same time, the Czech firm of Skoda received a separate contract to develop a gun capable of firing the same ammunition as the *sIG 33*.

Photographs of models of the new *15 cm sIG auf Panzerkampfwagen IV - Fahrgestell* were shown to Hitler on 7 February 1943. Hitler expressed the desire to see the first 40 vehicles by 12 May 1943 at the latest; 20 additional vehicles would follow.

Skoda completed 6 of the new *15 cm Sturmhaubitze 43 L/12* in March, 40 in April and 14 in May. Unofficially, the vehicle was listed as the *Gerät 581, Sturmpanzerwagen 604/16 (Alkett sIG auf PzKpfw IV mit kardanischer Aufhängung* (Cardan superstructure). It bore the *Sonderkraftfahrzeug* (special-purpose vehicle) number of *166*.

By April 1943 Hitler had directed that the new weapon would be placed under the purview of the Inspector General of the *Panzergruppe, Generaloberst* Guderian. Fifty of the new vehicles were to be issued to the field and ten of them were to be withheld as replacement vehicles. They were only to be used as determined by Hitler.

Hitler himself directed in a conference in May 1943 that this newly developed weapon would bear the designation of *Sturmpanzer* (assault tank). Up to now, the vehicle was also referred to as the *Sturmpanzer Brummbär* (Grizzly Bear). The designation *Brummbär* for the *Sturmpanzer 43* was not used by German forces. It first surfaced in an Allied intelligence bulletin (DTD Report 3066), but the source of that designation is not given. In the *Wehrmacht*, the vehicle was simply referred to as a *Sturmpanzer* or *Stupa* for short.

The new superstructure for the vehicles delivered from the *Nibelungenwerk* was mounted at the army maintenance depot in Vienna. The Austrian firms of Sauer and Simmering-Graz-Pauker assisted the depot in that. An initial series of 60 vehicles was completed in 1943, with 20 being constructed in April and the remaining 40 in May. A *Sturmpanzer* was demonstrated for Hitler on 14 May 1943.

All of the vehicles of the initial production run were issued to the newly formed *Sturmpanzer-Abteilung 216*. They were used for the first time - with success - during Operation Citadel. The only disadvantage to the vehicle was the excessive strain placed on the *Panzer IV* chassis due to the extra weight. That led to constant problems with the running gear and the final drives.

Despite that, the vehicle proved itself in the following months of employment at the front. As a result, Hitler personally ordered that production of the *Sd.Kfz. 166* be taken up again with a monthly output of 20 vehicles. The second series of vehicles was started in December 1943. In the process, a number of improvements were incorporated into the vehicles. Despite that, the strain on the running gear and drive train continued to be a problem.

It was decided at the end of January 1944 to stop the production of the second series with 60 vehicles. That would allow time to observe how well the new running gear with rubber-cushioned, steel-rimmed roadwheels would perform.

Additional changes, especially in the driver's area, were introduced with the third series of vehicles. In addition, Skoda was directed to reduce the weight of the 15 cm *Sturmhaubitze 43* (model 43 assault howitzer). That could basically be achieved only by reducing the armor on the vehicle. The physical appearance of the vehicle remained virtually unchanged. The modified howitzer received the designation of *Sturmhaubitze 43/1*.

Units in the field requested additional improvements to the vehicle, to include a better ability to defend the vehicle against enemy hunter/killer teams and installing a *MG 34* in a ball mount. Those suggestions as well as others led to a complete reworking of the superstructure in the first half of 1944. The "new" *Sturmpanzer 43* was produced in a fourth series of vehicles by the *Deutsche Eisenwerke* in Duisburg until March 1945.

According to the *Waffenamt* (weapons directorate), the following numbers of vehicles were produced"

April 1943	20
May 1943	40
June 1943	--
August 1943	--
September 1943	--
October 1943	--
November 1943	--
December 1943	10
January 1944	20
February 1944	15
March 1944	16
April 1944	12
May 1944	3
June 1944	40
July 1944	30
August 1944	20
September 1944	19
October 1944	14
November 1944	3
December 1944	23
January 1945	1
February 1945	13

The *Waffenamt* noted the following numbers of vehicles in inventory (minus frontline losses) as follows:

1 January 1944	31
1 July 1944	163
1 December 1944	184

Sturmpanzer 43 (first series)

Sixty vehicles were produced in the initial production series. To construct the vehicles, 8 *Panzer IV, Ausführung E* and *F* chassis and 52 *Panzer IV, Ausführung G* chassis were provided.

The chassis of the *Panzer IV, Ausführung E* and *F* were used in an unmodified condition, i.e., the armor on the hull side and the longer muffler were retained. Ventilator covers were screwed on to the brake maintenance covers, identical to those used on the *Panzer III*. An additional 30-mm armor plate was affixed to the front slope of both chassis. In addition, new cooling and ventilation covers were mounted, identical to those used on the *Panzer IV, Ausführung G*.

The smoke-grenade launchers were removed. In the case of the *Panzer IV, Ausführung E* that was in the middle of the hull; for the *Ausführung F* that was on the left-hand side. The vertical-mounting bracket for the smoke-grenade launchers was not removed, however.

The gas-electric auxiliary *DKW* motor for traversing the turret, which was housed in the engine compartment, was removed. The exhaust opening for the *DKW* motor, located in the rear of the hull, was welded shut with a square plate.

The superstructure of the original tank, including the turret, was removed. Only the covering for the engine compartment remained. The new superstructure was constructed over the then open area.

The driver received an armored, slightly extended bay position, into which a *Fahrersehklappe 80* (model 80 driver vision block) was incorporated. It was the same type of driver vision block used on the *Tiger I*. To the left of the driver's station was a cap that covered the end of the ventilation pipe of the brake housing.

The 15-cm *Sturmhaubitze 43* was located above and slightly to the right of the driver's position, where it was installed in the 100-mm thick front slope. The gun had a ball mounting which protected the howitzer and a short length of armor protected the gun barrel.

A pistol port was located to the rear of the superstructure on each side. An armored plug was secured to the interior of the fighting compartment by a chain; the plug could be pushed out from the inside.

The rear wall of the armored superstructure had a two-piece crew hatch. To the right and the left on the rear outside wall of the fighting compartment were two welded armored covers that opened to the bottom. These protected the fighting compartment ventilators. On the top side of the armored containers were antenna mounts that allowed various types of radio antennas to be mounted. Ventilation channels were mounted on the left- and right-hand side of the fighting compartment roof. They started with the end of the howitzer. It was intended for the channels to draw out the heavy fumes that developed when the howitzer was fired.

There were three hatches built into the roof of the fighting compartment. The gun commander had a round one, while the loader and the gunner each had square ones. There was an opening in the gunner's hatch. It housed the gun optics, the *Selbstfahrlafetten-Zielfernrohr 1a* (model 1a self-propelled gun optic). The loader's hatch also possessed an opening. It enabled the mounting of a *MG 34* when it was positioned up. It was identical to the mounting used on a *Sturmgeschütz III, Ausführung G*.

Behind the fighting compartment on the right-hand side of the vehicle was a large container for vehicular basic-issue items. In addition, two brackets for holding replacement roadwheels were welded to the rear of the fighting compartment.

During the *Führer* conference of 6 March 1943, it was ordered that all armored vehicles were to be outfitted with sideskirts. Because that directive also applied to the *Sturmpanzer*, sideskirt brackets were also welded to *Sturmpanzer* whenever the opportunity arose.

Sturmpanzer 43 (second series)

It was planned to eliminate deficiencies noted in the initial production series of vehicles when the second series was started in December 1943. The *Sturmpanzer 43* of the second series made use of the basically unmodified chassis of the *Panzer IV, Ausführung H*, which was then currently in production. As with the first series, the *DKW* auxiliary engine was removed and the exhaust port welded over. The fighting compartment superstructure was retained with little modification, however, the number of pistol ports was increased to two per side. The gun-barrel armor was lengthened.

The roof of the fighting compartment was changed and the number of hatches reduced to two. The gun commander's two-piece, round hatch was retained, as was the two-piece, square hatch of the loader. The two-piece gunner's hatch was eliminated. The gunner's optics was routed through a small opening above his station that was protected by a movable plate that moved along a track. Because the protective covering extended over the front of the superstructure at certain firing angles, a piece of metal was affixed to the superstructure front in the respective area to provide additional protection.

Because the ventilation of the fighting compartment did not work well in the first production series, a new ventilator was installed on the roof of the fighting compartment in lieu of the ventilation channels. As a result, both of the armored ventilator covers at the back of the fighting compartment were eliminated. There was also only provision for one antenna; it was located on the right-hand side.

Angle iron was welded onto the top of the fighting compartment roof in front of the forward-opening gun commander's hatch and in front of and on the forward-opening loader's hatch. These were designed to cause rounds to ricochet away from the hatch openings.

An armor plate was affixed to the area beneath the *Fahrersehklappe 80* at the driver's station to help prevent rounds from penetrating into the weak area of the superstructure between the driver's station and the fighting compartment.

The large basic-issue-item container was moved to the left-hand side of the vehicle. In some photographs, one can see an intermediate filter on the right rear track guard that was identical to the one used on the *Panzer IV, Ausführung H*.

Two additional mounting brackets for replacement roadwheels were also affixed to the rear of the engine compartment. Armor plating was placed around the muffler. The heavy roads of the main gun could be placed there while reloading the vehicle.

Based on soldier complaints from the field, newly designed triangle-shaped mounting brackets for the sideskirts were placed on all *Panzer IV* vehicles starting in October 1943. The previously used mounting brackets were poorly designed and led to the loss of sideskirts. These new mountings were also applied to the second production series of the *Sturmpanzer 43*.

Finally, all of the vehicles received a base coat of *Zimmerit*, the anti-magnetic mine coating.

Sturmpanzer 43 (first series - modified)

About half of the first series of the *Sturmpanzer 43* - 30 of the 60 vehicles - were brought back with *Sturmpanzer-Abteilung 216* when it was pulled out of the line on the Eastern Front. They were overhauled at the army maintenance depot in Vienna and modified to second series standards.

The roof of the modified fighting compartment was identical to those of the second series, however, the armored ventilator covers at the rear were left in place.

In cases where the original chassis was from a *Panzer IV, Ausführung E*, newer standardized parts were incorporated during the overhaul, e.g., the elimination of the long exhaust muffler and the replacement of the brake maintenance access panels.

The sideskirt mounting brackets were replaced with the new triangular type. Finally, a coat of *Zimmerit* was applied to all of these vehicles.

Organization and Employment of the *Sturmpanzer* Battalions
Sturmpanzer-Abteilung 216

The formation of the first *Sturmpanzer* battalion, *Sturmpanzer-Abteilung 216*, was directed at the end of April 1943. The battalion was organized with a headquarters, a headquarters company, three *Sturmpanzer* companies, the headquarters *Sturmpanzer* section and a maintenance platoon. In accordance with it *Kriegsstärkenachweisung* (tables of organization and equipment), the battalion had 45 *Sturmpanzer*.

All of the battalion personnel were moved to Amiens at the beginning of May, where intensive training began as soon as the new equipment arrived. At this time, *schweres Panzerjäger-Regiment 656* was formed for Operation Citadel. *Sturmpanzer-Abteilung 216* was assigned to it as its third battalion, where it was redesignated as the *III./schweres Panzerjäger-Regiment 656*.

Starting on 10 June 1943, the *III./schweres Panzerjäger-Regiment 656* was transported to *Heeresgruppe Mitte* (Army Group Center). At the end of June, the regiment was staged in its attack positions not far from the Orel - Kursk rail line. On 5 July 1943, Operation Citadel was launched. The *III./schweres Panzerjäger-Regiment 656* was employed there for all of July. At the beginning of August, it was moved to a rest area in the vicinity of Briansk with its remaining 18 *Sturmpanzer*. At the end of August, it was moved further back to Dnepropetrowsk.

At Dnepropetrowsk the necessary repairs and maintenance on the *Sturmpanzer* were conducted at the Tritosnaja tank factory. Starting 10 September 1943, the battalion was constantly engaged during the fighting for the bridgehead at Saporoshe, which had to be abandoned on 15 October. During this time period, the battalion reverted to its original designation of *Sturmpanzer-Abteilung 216*.

After a fighting retreat, *Sturmpanzer-Abteilung 216* reached Nikopol, where it participated in the defensive fighting for the bridgehead along with the *Ferdinande* of *schwere Panzerjäger-Abteilung 653*.

As a result of the losses and the necessity for major overhaul on the remaining serviceable vehicles within both battalions, they were pulled out of frontline service starting in the middle of December 1943. They were pulled back to the boundaries of the *Reich* and overhauled at the army maintenance facility at Vienna.

As a result of the Allied landings at Anzio/Nettuno at the end of January 1944, the expedited movement of the battalion to the Italian beachheads was ordered. Starting in February, the *Sturmpanzer* of the battalion were employed along with the *Tigers* of *schwere Panzer-Abteilung 508* and the *Panthers* of *Panzer-Regiment 26*.

After that fighting, the battalion was moved to the area around Pisa to be refitted. At the end of May it was once again sent in the direction of Rome. It was possible to temporarily halt the advance of the enemy east of the Italian capital. Following that was a continuous fighting retreat with short pauses for necessary maintenance.

At the time there was also a *4./Sturmpanzer-Abteilung 216*. It had been formed in the spring of 1944. The company was detached from the battalion in September, however, to help form the basis for the establishment of *Sturmpanzer-Abteilung 219*.

At the end of 1944 the battalion was in the area around Bologna, where it helped prevent the breakthrough of the Allies into the Po Valley. After the advance of the Allies came to a halt in the winter of 1944/1945, they used the opportunity to reconstitute their forces. At the beginning of April 1945, the Allied offensive started against the German positions in the Po Valley. At the time, *Sturmpanzer-Abteilung 216* had 42 operational *Sturmpanzer*. However, in the course of the subsequent withdrawals towards Lake Garda, all of them were either combat losses or had to be blown up to prevent their capture by the Allies.

Kriegsgliederung der Sturmpanzer—Abteilung 216 ("III./Panzer—Regiment 656") Stand: 07.1943

Stab

1.Kp.

Kompanietrupp

1.Zug

2.Zug

3.Zug

2.Kp.

Kompanietrupp

1.Zug

© Trojca 2001. / M.Jaugitz

Kriegsgliederung der Sturmpanzer-Abteilung 216 ("III./Panzer-Regiment 656") Stand: 07.1943

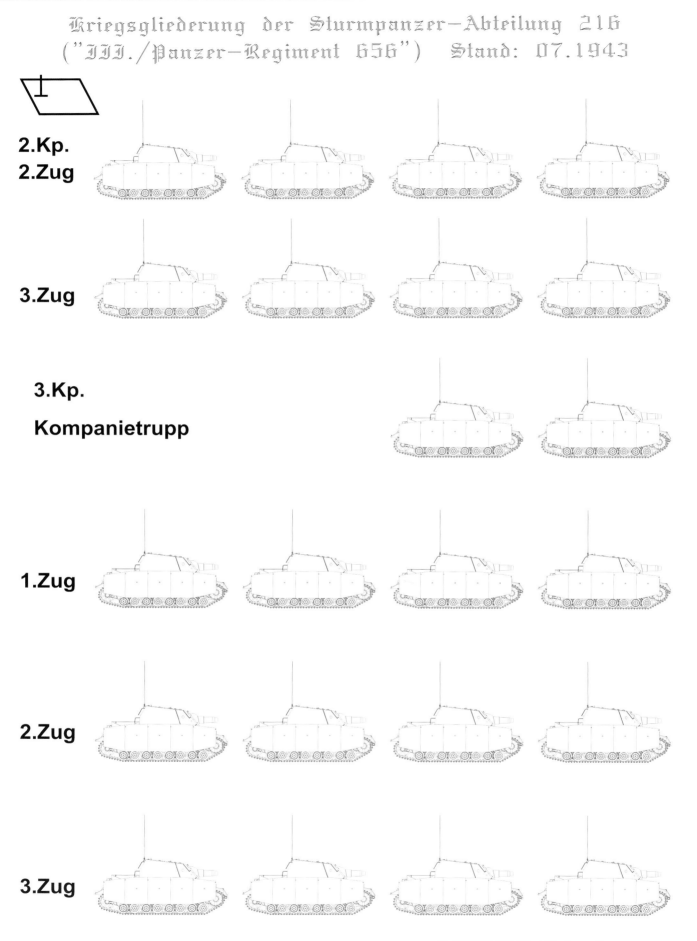

2.Kp.
2.Zug

3.Zug

3.Kp.

Kompanietrupp

1.Zug

2.Zug

3.Zug

Photographs

001. A brand-new *Sturmpanzer* (command vehicle with two antennas). The bolted-on additional armor can be seen to good advantage. The folding mounting ladder for the crew can be seen on the left-hand side behind the driver's compartment.

002. This *Sturmpanzer* (command vehicle) has already been equipped with sideskirts. The vehicle was constructed using a *Panzer IV, Ausführung E* chassis. Note the ventilator covers that were also used on the *Panzer III*.

003. The first brand-new *Sturmpanzer* were released to *Sturmpanzer-Abteilung 216* at the beginning of May 1943. These vehicles do not have any camouflage paint.

004. After partisans had blown up this stretch of rail line, this transport train derailed. In the process, a *Sturmpanzer* flipped over.

005. The *Sturmpanzer* are prepared for the offensive.

006. At the beginning of operation Citadel the *Sturmpanzer* supported the *Ferdinande* of *schweres Panzer-Regiment 656*.

007. *Major* Kahl, the commander of *Sturmpanzer-Abteilung 216*.

008. Situation briefing! The Roman *III* identifies this *Sturmpanzer* as belonging to the battalion headquarters *Sturmpanzer* section.

009. Another vehicle of the headquarters *Sturmpanzer* section. *Sturmpanzer II* was destroyed in the first few days of the attack.

010. The numeral *52* has also been painted on the armored ventilation protectors of the rear of the fighting compartment.

011. *Sturmpanzer 52* was put on display in Moscow after having been captured.

012. Two *Sturmpanzer* in an assembly area. A tarpaulin has been placed on the main gun ball mount to protect against dust.

013. This *Sturmpanzer* - built on the chassis of a *Panzer IV, Ausführung E* - has also had a tarpaulin placed on the fighting compartment and the assault howitzer to protect it against the elements.

014. A *Sturmpanzer* moved in a wooded area to its attack position.

015. Maintenance. This *Sturmpanzer* has been built on the chassis of a *Panzer IV, Ausführung E*. An indicator of that is the vertical flat piece of metal mounted on the left-hand side of the rear hull of the vehicle. It was used as a mounting bracket for the smoke-grenade launcher.

016. A *Sd.Kfz. 166* is loaded with ammunition. The 38-kilogram rounds are transferred from the ammunition carrier to the rear deck of the *Sturmpanzer*.

017. A break in the action. The left-hand sideskirts are missing on this *Sturmpanzer*. A *Panzer IV, Ausführung E* was also used in making this *Sturmpanzer*.

018 and 019. *Sturmpanzer 28* has received several hits on its sideskirts and on the superstructure. The crew is happy that none of the rounds penetrated.

020. This *Sturmpanzer*, on the other hand, was less lucky. An artillery round has severely damaged the fighting compartment of the vehicle.

021. Ambush position! The chassis number of 82903 has been painted above the driver's vision optics - the *Fahrersehklappe 80*.

022. *Panzerschütze* Feldt in front of his *Sturmpanzer*. The front folding mudguard has been torn away. The thickness of the bolted-on additional armor can clearly be seen.

023. The rear *Rollenwagen* has been removed. The *Anschlagbock*, however, was not dismounted.

024. Numerous hits on the side of this *Sd.Kfz. 166* have rendered it non-operational.

025. *Sturmpanzer 30* has a striking camouflage pattern.

026. This *Sturmhaubitze 43* has been fitted with a muzzle protector. A tow cable mount has been placed on the cover to the differential.

027. Movement before operational deployment.

028. This *Sturmpanzer* - also based on a *Panzer IV, Ausführung E* chassis - has a tarpaulin placed on it to protect it against the weather.

029. A maintenance facility in the woods. Two 18-ton prime movers can be seen next to the *Sturmpanzer*. One of the prime movers has a *Bilstein* crane.

030. Vehicles constantly became disabled due to the great demands placed on them and their continuous employment. The area most commonly affected was the chassis, since it had to support more weight than it was originally designed to do.

031. A rain guard has been mounted on this vehicle above the *Fahrersehklappe 80*.

032. A disabled *Sturmpanzer* is being evacuated on a *Sonder-Anhänger 116*.

033. The *Sturmpanzer* were pulled out of the front lines in December 1943…

034. …and transported to Vienna on flat cars.

035. Small *Kampfgruppen* of *Sturmpanzer-Abteilung 216* were employed in the bridgehead at Nikopol.

036. Because recovery vehicles were not available in sufficient quantities, damaged vehicles frequently had to be towed by operational ones. *Sturmpanzer 1* is seen here towing *Sturmpanzer 3*.

037. In the middle of February 1944, 28 *Sturmpanzer* were moved to Italy in response to the Allied landings at Anzio and Nettuno.

038. The *Zimmerit* coating has been applied to the vehicles. Here we see a vehicle of the second production series.

039. The final drives have been taken out of *Sturmpanzer 16*. A felt air filter has been fastened to the vehicle on the right rear track guard.

040. Operations at Littoria (near Nettuno). A *Bergewanne III* can be seen between the *Sturmpanzer*.

041. Most of the buildings in the surrounding area have been destroyed. The rubble makes it difficult for the vehicles to advance.

042. This *Sturmpanzer* awaiting repairs has also been fitted with a felt filter.

043. This *Sturmpanzer* is a modified version of the first production series. Only one submachine gun port is visible on the fighting compartment.

044 and 045. Frontal views of the *Sturmpanzer*. This vehicle has a coating of *Zimmerit* applied. An armor plate has been mounted below the *Fahrersehklappe 80*.

046. Mounts for four spare roadwheels were mounted on the rear deck of vehicles of the second production series.

047. Additional armor has also been bolted on to the lower part of the front slope of this *Sturmpanzer*.

048. The barrel of the *Sturmhaubitze 43* and the 38-kilogram round.

049. A member of *Sturmpanzer-Abteilung 216* in front of his vehicle.

050. Another modified *Sturmpanzer* of the first production series. The armored ventilator protectors were not removed. A number of rounds have been placed on the rear deck that still have to be stowed inside the vehicle.

051. In a firing position.

052. The crew of *Sturmpanzer II* of *Sturmpanzer-Abteilung 216* takes a short break.

053. An 18-ton prime mover recovers a disabled vehicle.

054. and 055. This modified *Sturmpanzer* of the first production series (chassis number 80976) was captured by the Allies during the fighting in Italy and extensively examined. When the first production series vehicles were overhauled, most of the old components were exchanged, so that an exact identification is difficult. It is hard to tell that this *Sturmpanzer* was originally constructed using the chassis of a *Panzer IV, Ausführung E*.

056. *Sturmpanzer-Abteilung 217*, which was formed in May and June of 1944 also received a few vehicles from the second production series.

057. This *Sturmpanzer* was constructed using the chassis of a *Panzer IV, Ausführung F*.

Photo 001

Photo 002

Photo 003

Photo 004

Photo 005

Photo 006

Photo 007

Photo 008

Photo 009

Photo 010

Photo 011

Photo 012

15

Photo 013

Photo 014

Photo 015

Photo 016

Photo 017

18

Photo 019

Photo 018

19

Photo 020

Photo 021

Photo 022

Photo 023

Photo 024

Photo 025

Photo 026

Photo 027

Photo 028

Photo 029

Photo 030

Photo 031

Photo 032

Photo 033

Photo 034

29

Photo 035

Photo 036

Photo 037

Photo 038

Photo 039

Photo 040

Photo 041

Photo 042

Photo 043

Photo 044

34

Photo 045

Photo 046

Photo 047

Photo 048

Photo 049

Photo 050

Photo 051

Photo 052

Photo 053

40

Photo 054

Photo 055

Photo 056

Photo 057

Early model Sd.Kfz.166 Sturmpanzer „Brummbär" at the Kubinka Museum, Russia

43

Early model Sd.Kfz.166 Sturmpanzer „Brummbär" at the Kubinka Museum, Russia

44

Early model Sd.Kfz.166 Sturmpanzer „Brummbär" at the Kubinka Museum, Russia

Early model Sd.Kfz.166 Sturmpanzer „Brummbär" at the Kubinka Museum, Russia

Early model Sd.Kfz.166 Sturmpanzer „Brummbär" at the Kubinka Museum, Russia

Early model Sd.Kfz.166 Sturmpanzer „Brummbär" at the Kubinka Museum, Russia

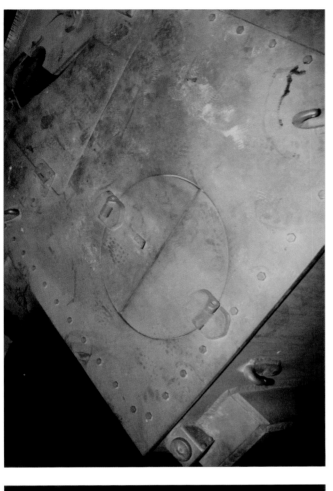

Early model Sd.Kfz.166 Sturmpanzer „Brummbär" at the Kubinka Museum, Russia

49

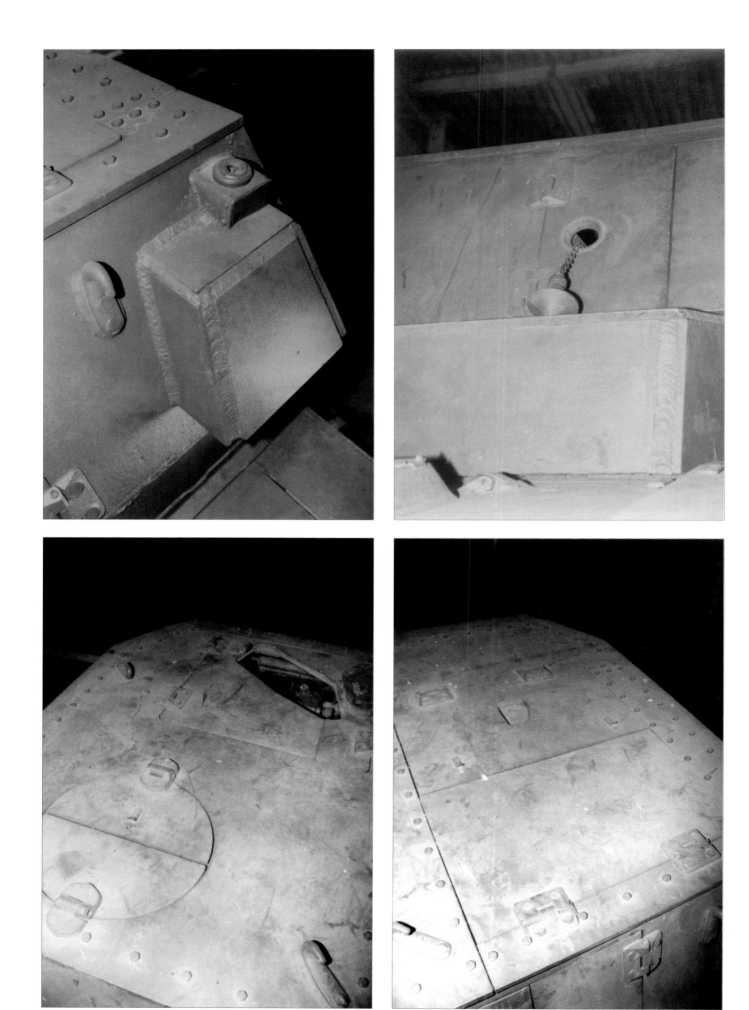

Early model Sd.Kfz.166 Sturmpanzer „Brummbär" at the Kubinka Museum, Russia

50

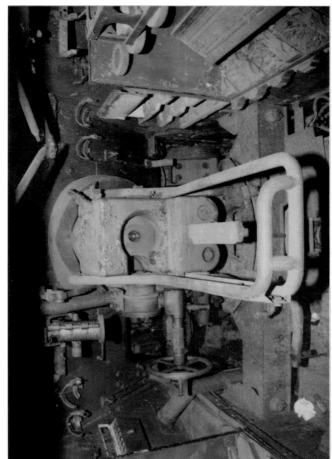

Early model Sd.Kfz.166 Sturmpanzer „Brummbär" at the Kubinka Museum, Russia

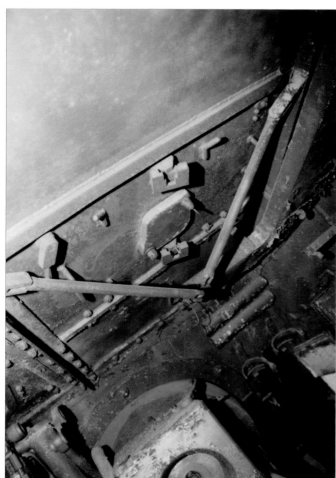

Early model Sd.Kfz.166 Sturmpanzer „Brummbär" at the Kubinka Museum, Russia

Early model Sd.Kfz.166 Sturmpanzer „Brummbär" at the Kubinka Museum, Russia

„ Sd.Kfz. 166 - Sturmpanzer", „ Sturmpanzer-Abteilung 216", 05.1943

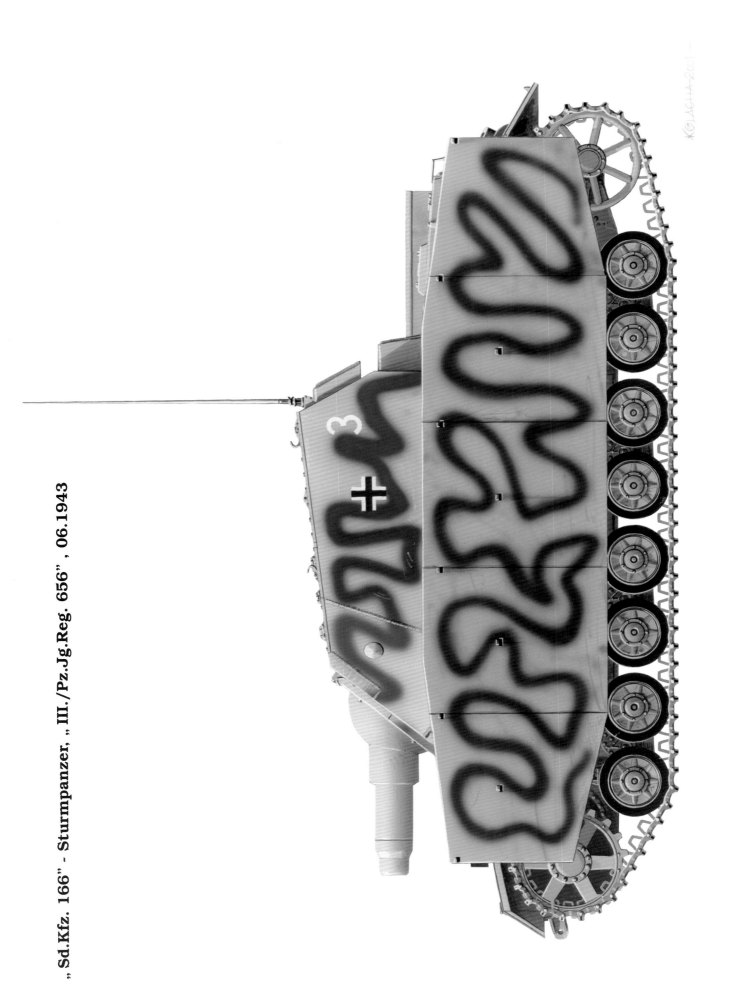

„ Sd.Kfz. 166" - Sturmpanzer, „ III./Pz.Jg.Reg. 656" , 06.1943

„ Sd.Kfz. 166" - Sturmpanzer „ III./Pz.Jg.Reg. 656" , 06.1943

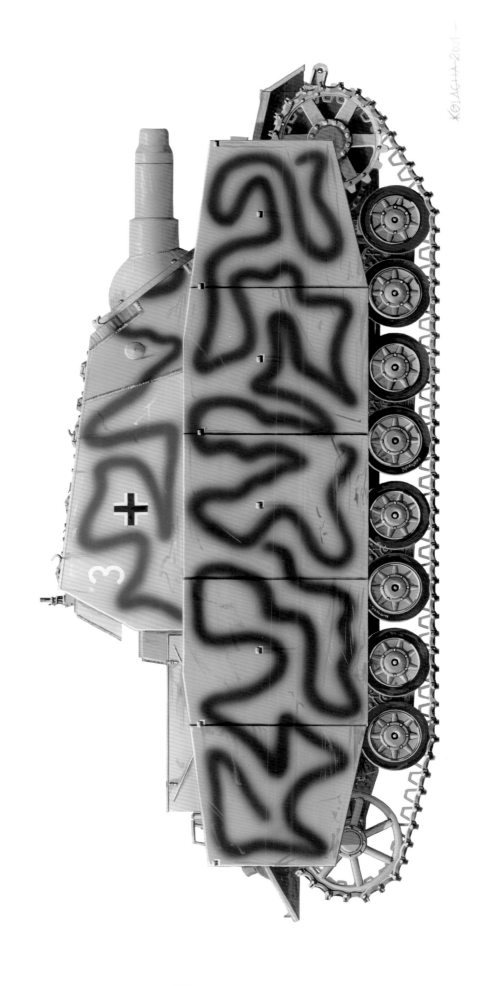

„ Sd.Kfz. 166" - Sturmpanzer „ III./Pz.Jg.Reg. 656" , 06.1943

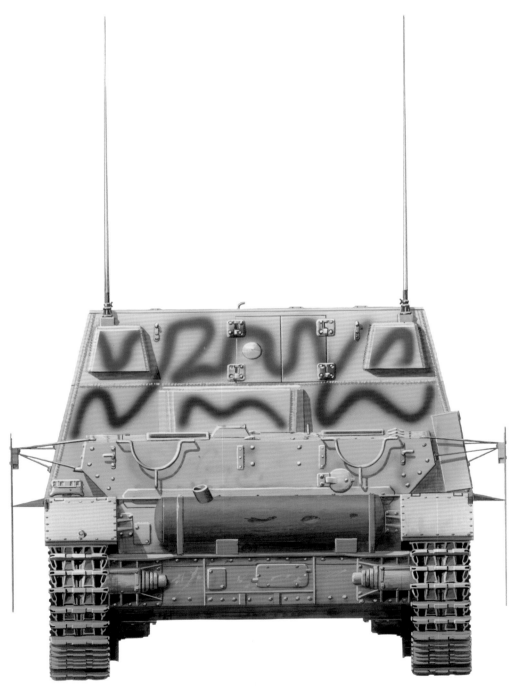

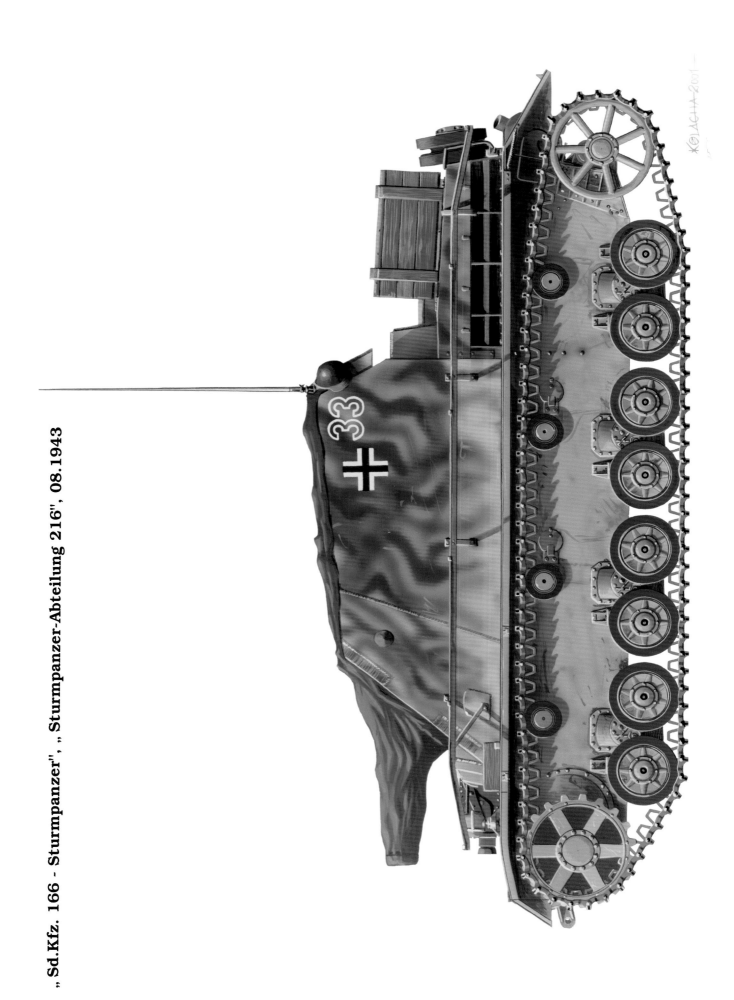

„Sd.Kfz. 166 - Sturmpanzer", „Sturmpanzer-Abteilung 216", 08.1943

„ Sd.Kfz. 166 - Sturmpanzer", „ Sturmpanzer-Abteilung 216", 10.1943

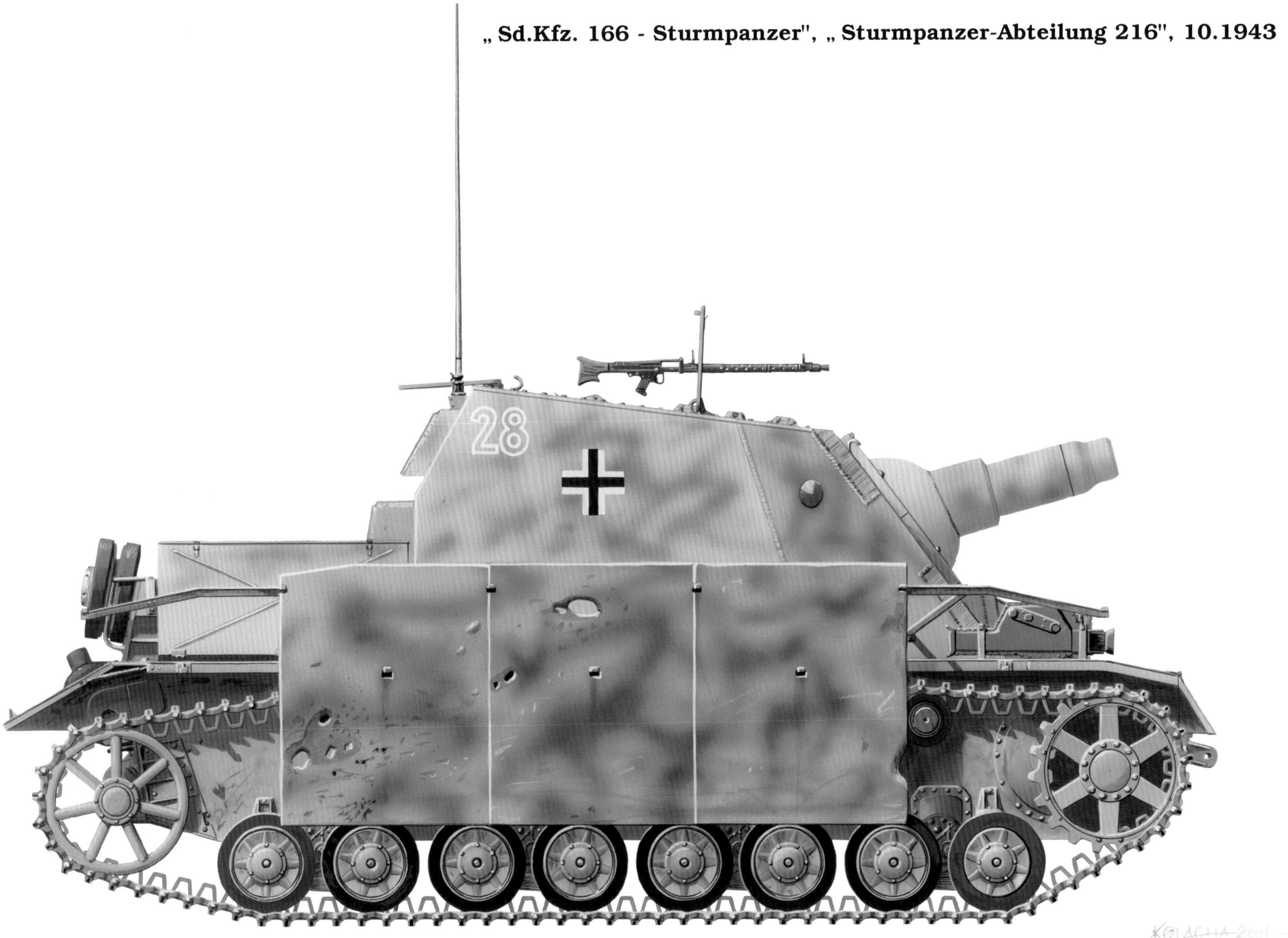

All drawings drawn to 1:35th scale.

(001) Sd. Kfz. 166 – STURMPANZER / © Trojca 2001

Left-hand side view of a *Sturmpanzer 43* (first production version), which was constructed on the chassis of a *Panzer IV, Ausführung E*. No tools have been added to the outside of the vehicle.

(002) Sd. Kfz. 166 – STURMPANZER / © Trojca 2001

Right-hand side view of a *Sturmpanzer 43* (first production version), which was constructed on the chassis of a *Panzer IV, Ausführung E*. No tools have been added to the outside of the vehicle.

(003)Sd. Kfz. 166 – STURMPANZER / © Trojca 2001

Right-hand side view of a *Sturmpanzer 43* (first production version), which was constructed on the chassis of a *Panzer IV, Ausführung E*.

(004) Sd. Kfz. 166 – STURMPANZER / © Trojca 2001

Left-hand side view of a *Sturmpanzer 43* (first production version), which was constructed on the chassis of a *Panzer IV, Ausführung E*. Mounting brackets for the sideskirts have been added to the vehicle.

(005) Sd. Kfz. 166 – STURMPANZER / © Trojca 2001

Top view of a *Sturmpanzer 43* (first production version), which was constructed on the chassis of a *Panzer IV, Ausführung E*.

(006) Sd. Kfz. 166 – STURMPANZER / © Trojca 2001

Top view of a *Sturmpanzer 43* (first production version), which was constructed on the chassis of a *Panzer IV, Ausführung E*. Mounting brackets for the sideskirts have been added to the vehicle.

(007) Sd. Kfz. 166 – STURMPANZER / © Trojca 2001

Left drawing: Frontal view of a *Sturmpanzer 43* (first production version), which was constructed on the chassis of a *Panzer IV, Ausführung E*. It has the ventilator covers that were also used on the *Panzer III*. Mounting brackets for the sideskirts have been added to the vehicle. Right drawing: Frontal view of a command version of the *Sturmpanzer 43* (first production version), which was constructed on the chassis of a *Panzer IV, Ausführung E*. Mounting brackets for the sideskirts have been added to the vehicle, as well as the sideskirts.

(008) Sd. Kfz. 166 – STURMPANZER / © Trojca 2001

Right-hand side view of a *Sturmpanzer 43* (first production version), which was constructed on the chassis of a *Panzer IV, Ausführung E*. Mounting brackets for the sideskirts have been added to the vehicle.

(009) Sd. Kfz. 166 – STURMPANZER / © Trojca 2001

Left drawing: Rear view of a *Sturmpanzer 43* (first production version), which was constructed on the chassis of a *Panzer IV, Ausführung E* with the long exhaust. Mounting brackets for the sideskirts have been added to the vehicle. Right drawing: Rear view of a command version of the *Sturmpanzer 43* (first production version), which was constructed on the chassis of a *Panzer IV, Ausführung E* with the long exhaust. Mounting brackets for the sideskirts have been added to the vehicle, as well as the sideskirts.

(010) Sd. Kfz. 166 – STURMPANZER / © Trojca 2001

Right-hand side view a *Sturmpanzer 43* (first production version), which was constructed on the chassis of a *Panzer IV, Ausführung E*. Mounting brackets for the sideskirts have been added to the vehicle, as well as the sideskirts. The howitzer has been elevated to its maximum elevation (+30°).

(011) Sd. Kfz. 166 – STURMPANZER / © Trojca 2001

Right-hand side view a *Sturmpanzer 43* (first production version), which was constructed on the chassis of a *Panzer IV, Ausführung E*. Mounting brackets for the sideskirts have been added to the vehicle, as well as the sideskirts.

(012) Sd. Kfz. 166 – STURMPANZER / © Trojca 2001

Top view of a *Sturmpanzer 43* (first production version), which was constructed on the chassis of a *Panzer IV*, *Ausführung E*. It has the ventilator covers of the *Panzer III*, as well as the long exhaust. Mounting brackets for the sideskirts have been added to the vehicle, as well as the sideskirts. The howitzer is deflected to the right to its maximum deflection.

(013) Sd. Kfz. 166 – STURMPANZER / © Trojca 2001

Right-hand side view of a *Sturmpanzer 43* (first production version), which was constructed on the chassis of a *Panzer IV*, *Ausführung F*. Mounting brackets for the sideskirts have been added to the vehicle. The howitzer is depressed to its maximum depression (-8°).

(014) Sd. Kfz. 166 – STURMPANZER / © Trojca 2001

Left drawing: Frontal view of a *Sturmpanzer 43* (first production version), which was constructed on the chassis of a *Panzer IV*, *Ausführung F*. It has additional armor welded to the hull sides. Mounting brackets for the sideskirts have been added to the vehicle. Right drawing: Frontal view of a *Sturmpanzer 43* (first production version), which was constructed on the chassis of a *Panzer IV*, *Ausführung F*. It has additional armor bolted on to the hull sides. Mounting brackets for the sideskirts have been added to the vehicle, as well as the sideskirts.

(015) Sd. Kfz. 166 – STURMPANZER / © Trojca 2001

Left-hand side view of a *Sturmpanzer 43* (first production version), which was constructed on the chassis of a *Panzer IV*, *Ausführung F*. Mounting brackets for the sideskirts have been added to the vehicle.

(016) Sd. Kfz. 166 – STURMPANZER / © Trojca 2001

Top view of a *Sturmpanzer 43* (first production version), which was constructed on the chassis of a *Panzer IV*, *Ausführung F*. Mounting brackets for the sideskirts have been added to the vehicle, as well as the sideskirts.

(017) Sd. Kfz. 166 – STURMPANZER / © Trojca 2001

Left drawing: Rear view of a *Sturmpanzer 43* (first production version), which was constructed on the chassis of a *Panzer IV*, *Ausführung F*. It has spare roadwheels in the roadwheel mounts. Mounting brackets for the sideskirts have been added to the vehicle, as well as the sideskirts. Tools for track work have been mounted next to the exhaust on the rear hull of the vehicle. Right drawing: Rear view of a command version of the *Sturmpanzer 43* (first production version), which was constructed on the chassis of a *Panzer IV*, *Ausführung F*. It does not have spare roadwheels in the roadwheel mounts. Mounting brackets for the sideskirts have been added to the vehicle, as well as the sideskirts.

(018) Sd. Kfz. 166 – STURMPANZER / © Trojca 2001

Right-hand side view of a command version of the *Sturmpanzer 43* (first production version), which was constructed on the chassis of a *Panzer IV*, *Ausführung F*. Mounting brackets for the sideskirts have been added to the vehicle, as well as some sideskirts. The forward hatch of the loader's station has been opened and a *MG 34* mounted.

(19, 20, 21, 22, 23 and 24) Sd. Kfz. 166 – STURMPANZER / © Trojca 2001

Details of the hull and the running gear of the *Panzer IV*, *Ausführung E* chassis (1:35, 1:17.5 and 1:10 scale).

(025) Sd. Kfz. 166 – STURMPANZER / © Trojca 2001

Thickness of the armor plates of the *Sturmpanzer*.

(001)
"Sd.Kfz. 166 – STURMPANZER"

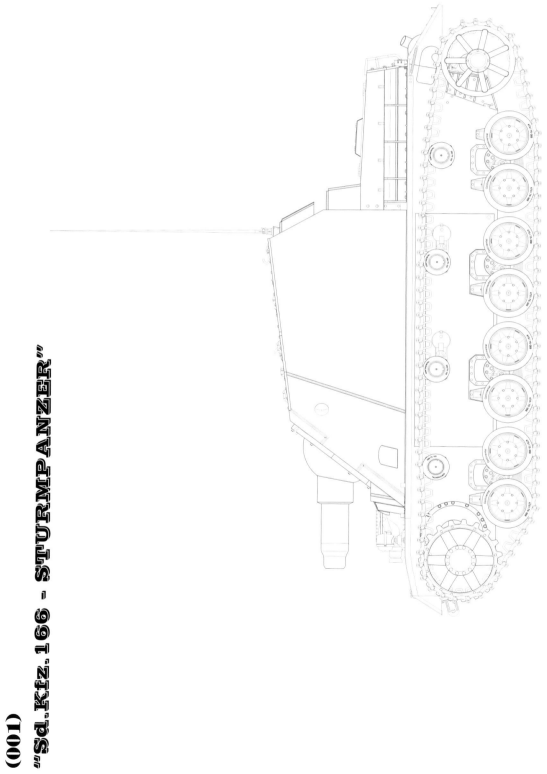

(002)
"Sd.Kfz. 166 – STURMPANZER"

© Trojca 2001.

© Trojca 2001.

(003)

"Sd.Kfz.166 - STURMPANZER"

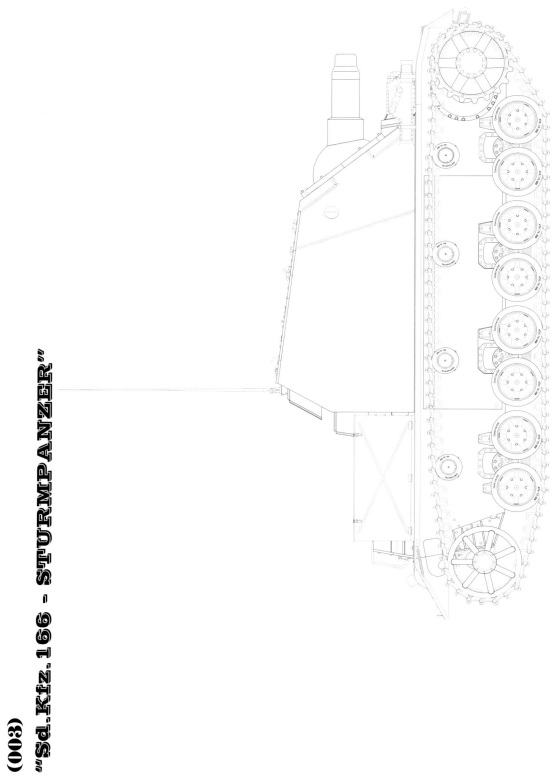

(004)

"Sd.Kfz.166 - STURMPANZER"

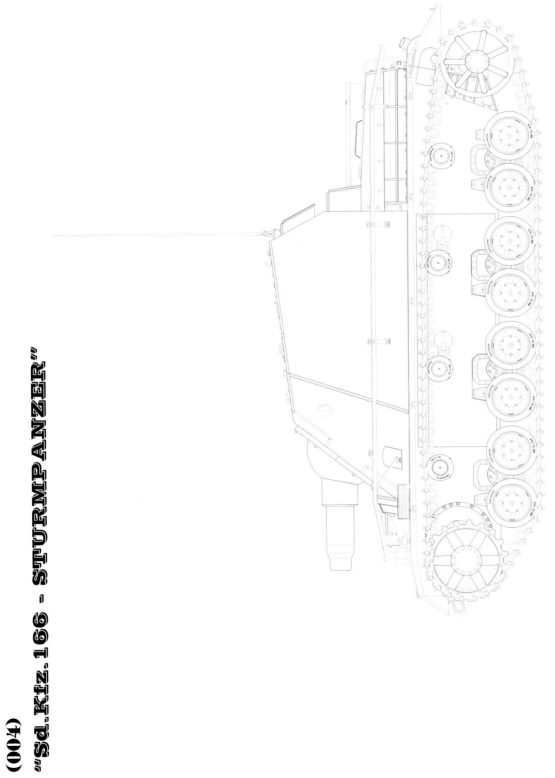

© Trojca 2001.

© Trojca 2001.

(005)
"Sd.Kfz. 166 - STURMPANZER"

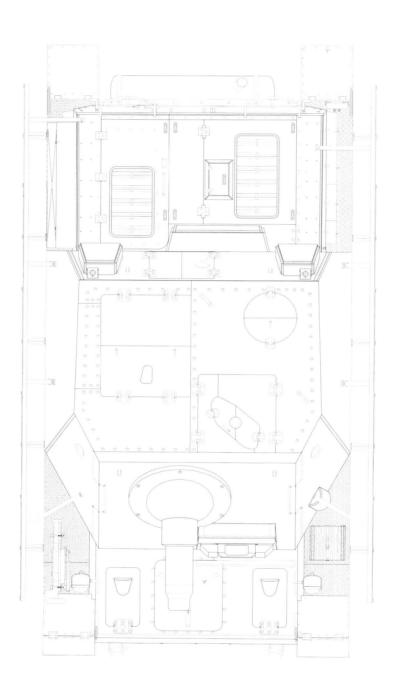

(006)

"Sd.Kfz.166 - STURMPANZER"

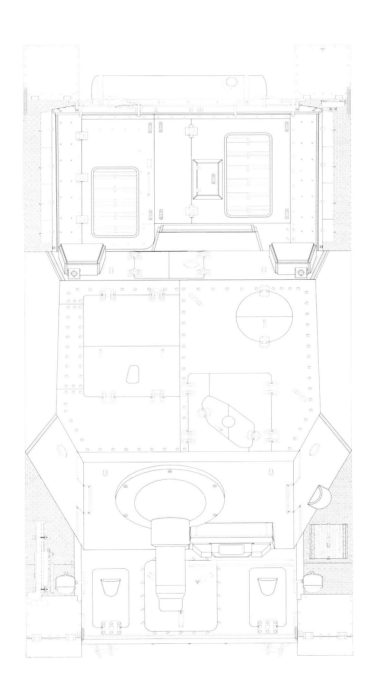

© Trojca 2001.

(007)

"Sd.Kfz.166 - STURMPANZER"

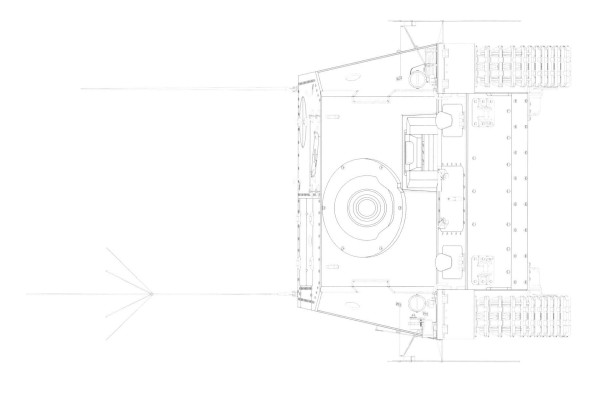

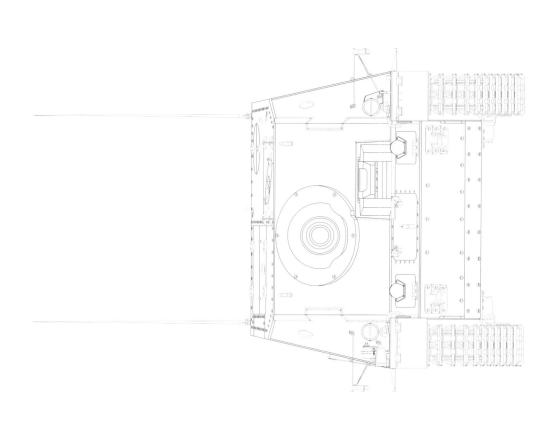

© Trojca 2001.

(008)

"Sd.Kfz. 166 - STURMPANZER"

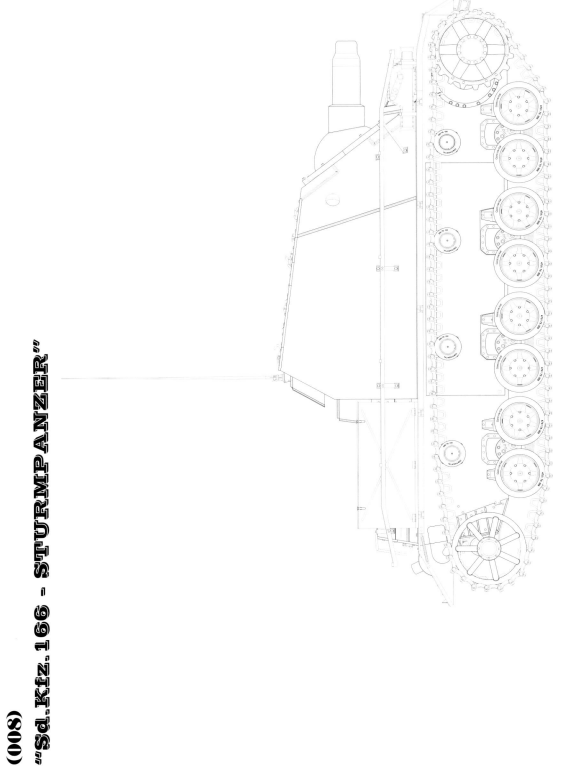

(009)

"Sd.Kfz. 166 - STURMPANZER"

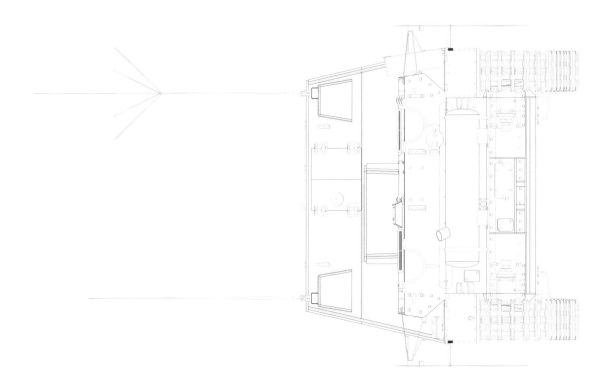

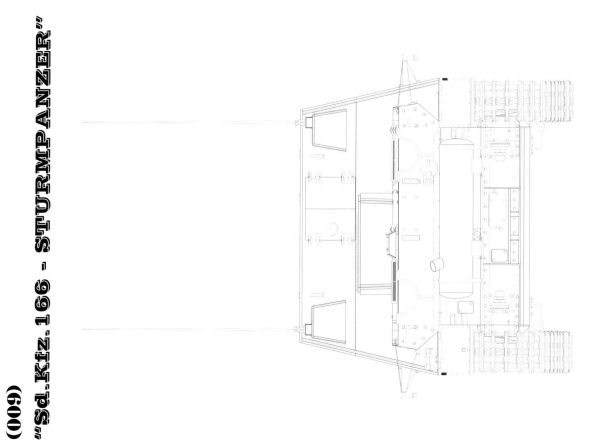

(010)
"Sd.Kfz.166 - STURMPANZER"

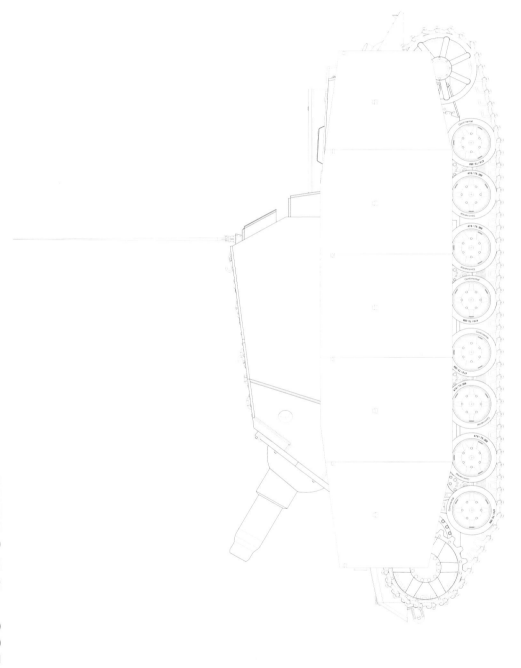

© Trojca 2001.

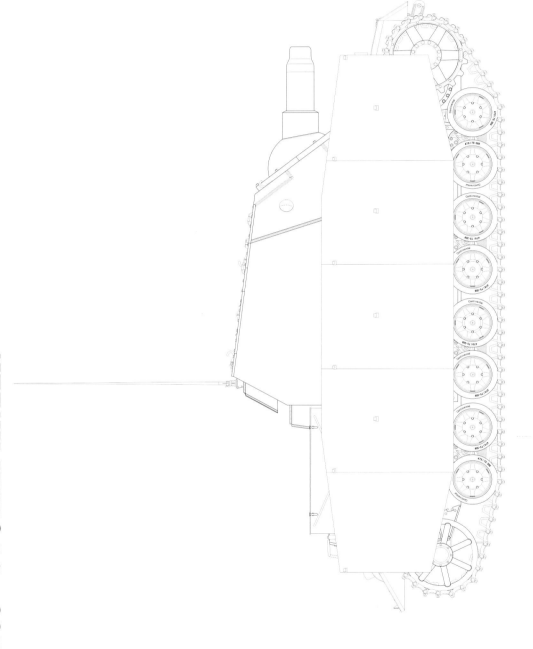

(011)
"Sd.Kfz. 166 – STURMPANZER"

© Trojca 2001.

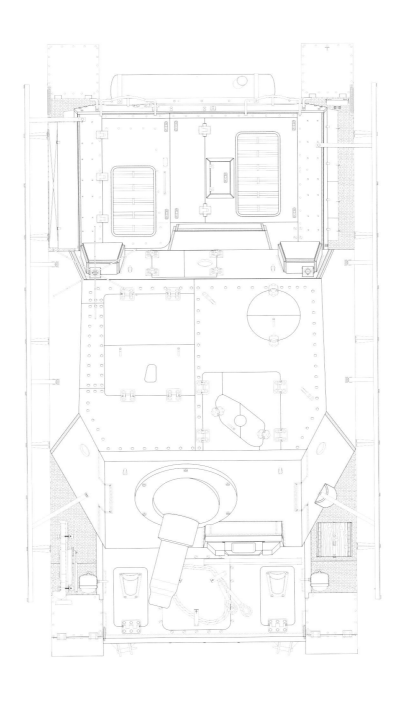

© Trojca 2001.

(013)
"Sd.Kfz. 166 - STURMPANZER"

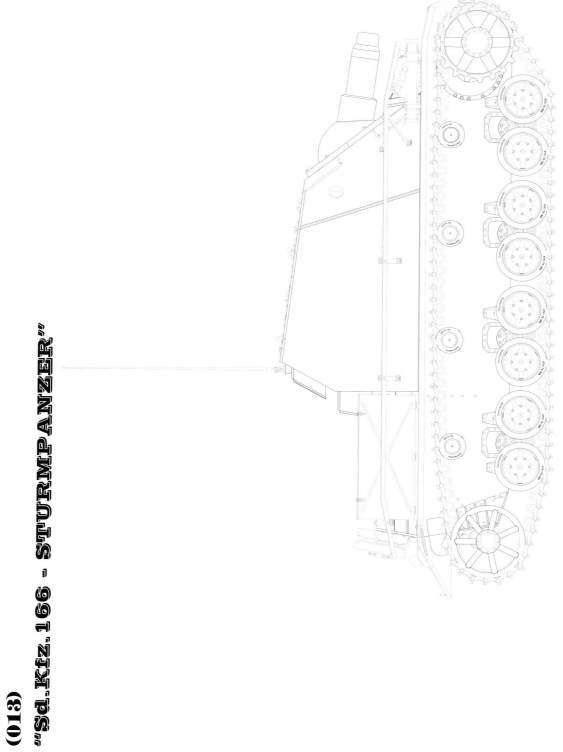

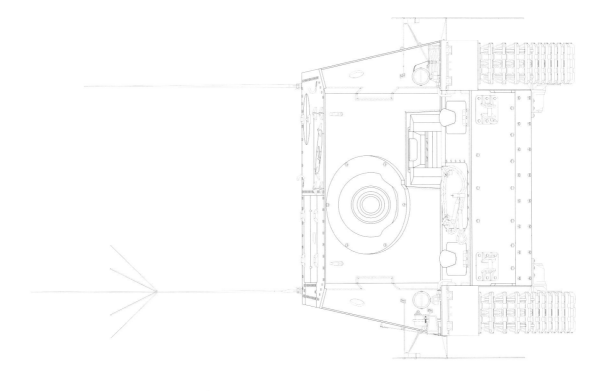

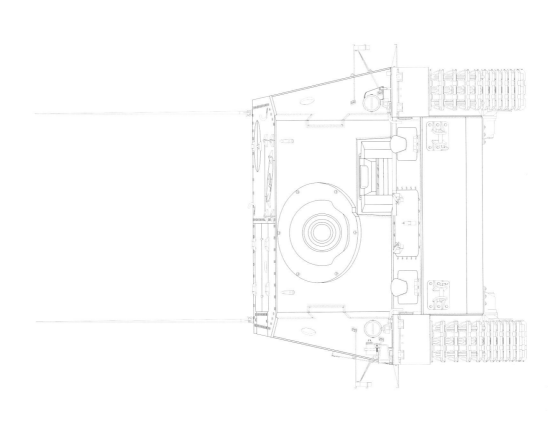

(014)
"Sd.Kfz. 166 - STURMPANZER"

© Trojca 2001.

(015)

"Sd.Kfz.166 - STURMPANZER"

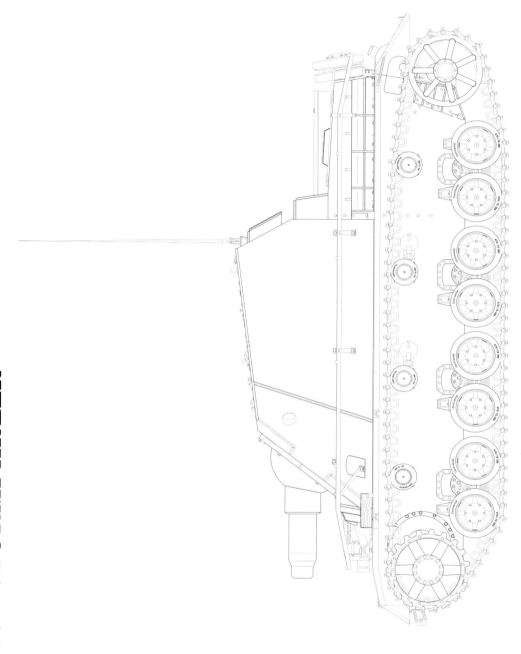

© Trojca 2001.

(016)

"Sd.Kfz.166 - STURMPANZER"

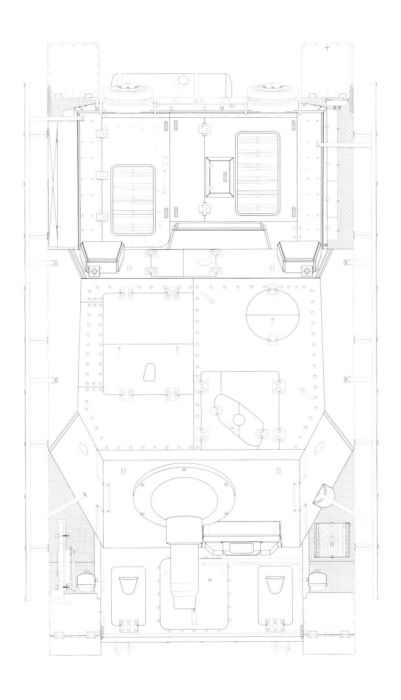

(017)
"Sd.Kfz. 166 – STURMPANZER"

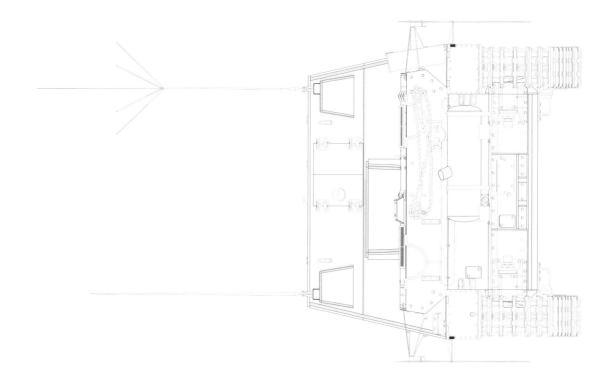

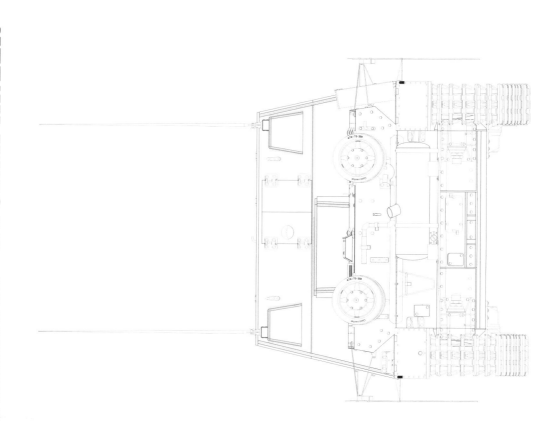

Trojca 2001.

© 3

(018)
"Sd.Kfz. 166 – STURMPANZER"

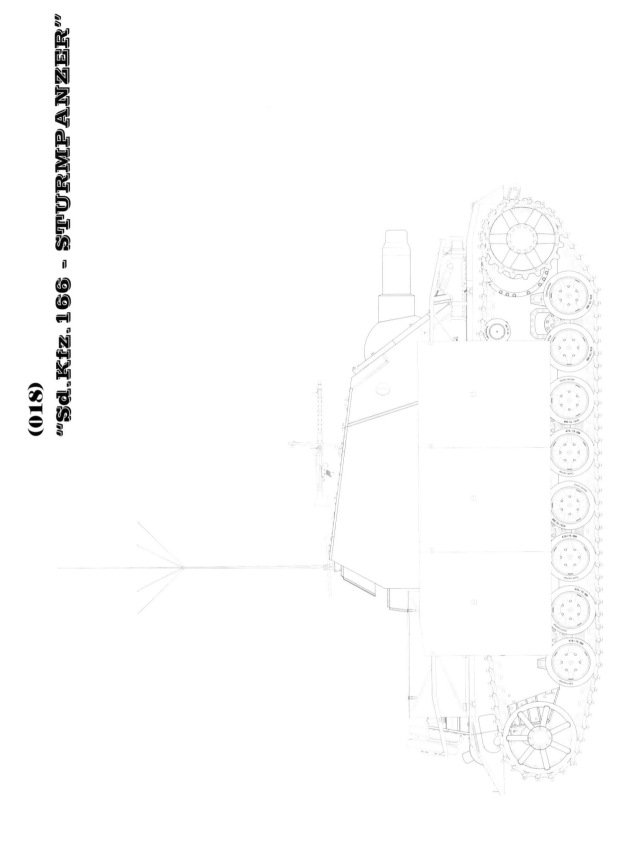

(019)

"Sd.Kfz. 166 - STURMPANZER"

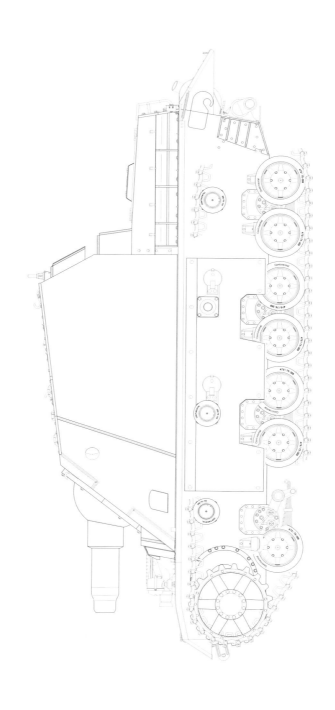

© Trojca 2001.

(020)

"Sd.Kfz.166 - STURMPANZER"

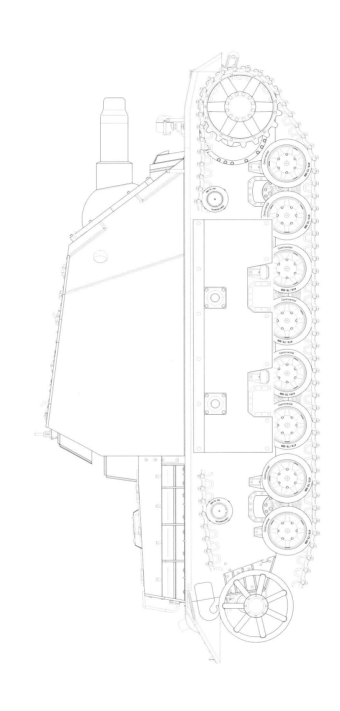

(021)
"Sd.Kfz.166 - STURMPANZER"

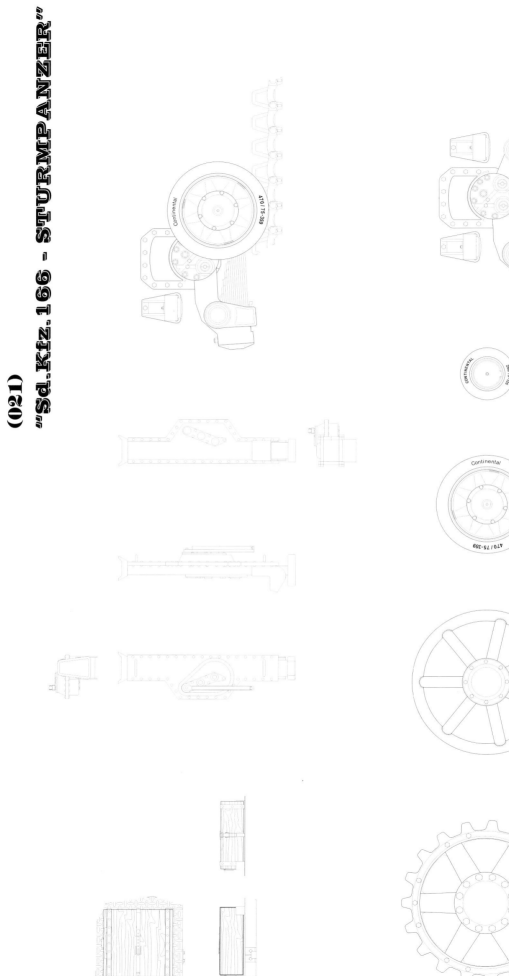

84

"Sd.Kfz. 166 - STURMPANZER"

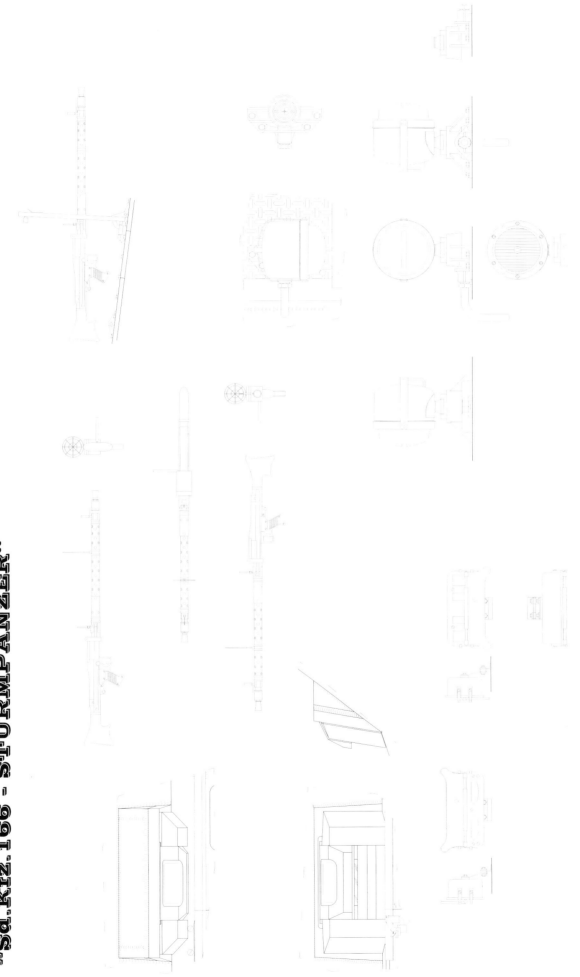

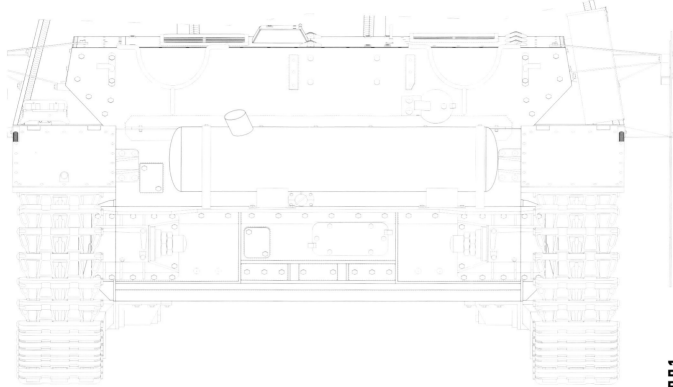

(023)
"Sd.Kfz.166 - STURMPANZER"

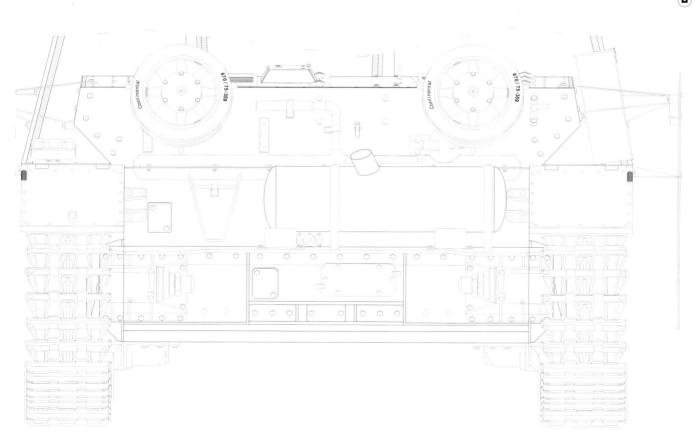

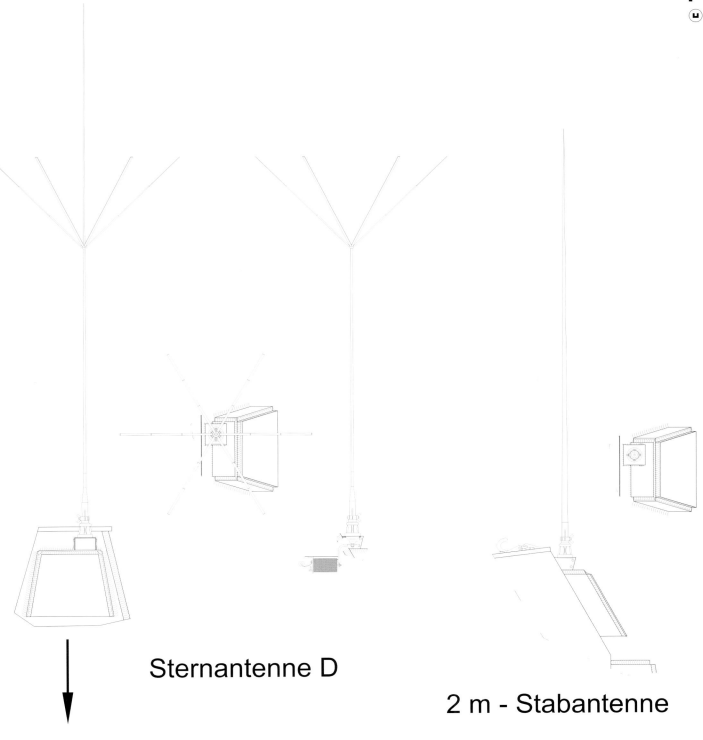

Sternantenne D

2 m - Stabantenne

(025)
"Sd.Kfz. 166 – STURMPANZER"

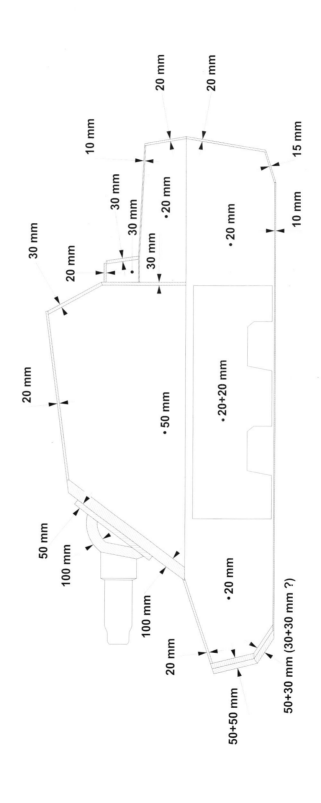